# Deepening the life of the Spirit

## resources for spiritual practice

First published in April 2012

© The Yearly Meeting of the Religious Society of Friends (Quakers) in Britain 2012

Developed by Ginny Wall

Published by Quaker Books, London

Designed by Quaker Communications Department, Friends House

Printed by RAP Spiderweb, Oldham

ISBN 978 1 907123 306

A free and continuing licence for the use of this copyright material is granted to Woodbrooke Quaker Study Centre

Britain Yearly Meeting of the Religious Society of Friends (Quakers) is a registered charity, number 1127633

# Preface

Quaker Life sees nurturing the spiritual life of Friends and meetings as being at the core of our thinking. We understand that who we are and what we do as Quakers flows from our spiritual lives, and is rooted in meeting for worship. We want to encourage all Friends and Quaker meetings to do whatever they can to help deepen their experience of the Spirit and engagement with each other.

'Deepening the life of the Spirit' became the focus for our Quaker Life Representative Council at Woodbrooke in April 2012. We offered nine workshops covering a variety of spiritual practices, ranging from walking meditation to sacred reading, given by Appleseed tutors, the Experiment with Light group, The Kindlers and Woodbrooke tutors. We also produced this book in collaboration with Woodbrooke to distribute to those attending the weekend and to all Quaker meetings. It contains brief guidance for a variety of practices that can help Friends deepen their experience of the Spirit (some covered at the weekend, some not), suggestions for finding out more about each practice, and a general book and links list.

At the same Representative Council, we launched a new book by Curt Gardner entitled *God just is: approaches to silent worship* (available from the Quaker Centre bookshop).

We hope that Friends and meetings will be encouraged to experiment with these ways of deepening our worshipping lives so that we can share, today, the transformative experience of the Spirit of God or inner light that has always been at the core of our tradition as Friends.

*Richard Summers, General Secretary Quaker Life*

# Contents

Acknowledgements

Introduction                                                                  1

Appleseed                                                                     5

Bible study                                                                   8

Body prayer                                                                  10

Centering down practices                                                     12

Centering Prayer: a practice of surrender                                    15

Experiment with Light                                                        17

Gratitude practices                                                          19

Journalling as spiritual practice                                            21

Listening prayer                                                             23

Mindfulness of breath                                                        25

A review of the day                                                          27

Sacred reading (lectio divina)                                               29

Sound and Light: healing relationships with the world and others            31

Spiritual friendship/companionship groups                                   34

Visualisation – imaginative prayer                                           37

Walking meditation                                                           40

Worship workshop guidelines                                                  42

Endnotes                                                                     47

Appendix: General resources for deepening the life of the Spirit            49

# Acknowledgements

Many people have contributed to the production of this book. Thanks are due to all who led workshops at the Quaker Life Representative Council held at Woodbrooke in April 2012, and who generously contributed guidance to practices for this book: Kathy Alton, Catherine King Ambler, Rex Ambler, Simon Best, Elizabeth Brown, Alec Davison, Brenda Heales, Frances Henley Lock, Pam Lunn, Stuart Masters, Helen Meads, Kathleen Nelson, Gill Pennington, Jasmine Piercy, Lizz Roe and Ginny Wall. Thanks also to all those in Quaker Life and the Quaker Communications Department of Britain Yearly Meeting for their work making the Representative Council happen and designing and printing this book.

# Introduction

Do you try to set aside times of quiet for openness to the Holy Spirit? All of us need to find a way into silence which allows us to deepen our awareness of the divine and to find the inward source of our strength. Seek to know an inward stillness, even amid the activities of daily life. Do you encourage in yourself and in others a habit of dependence on God's guidance for each day? Hold yourself and others in the Light, knowing that all are cherished by God.

*Advices & queries 3*

Living in the Spirit is like breathing. Spiritual practice is the in-breath while our loving action in the world is the out-breath. One flows from the other. So what happens when we do not attend to the in-breath? We begin to become short of breath, ill even. We may not notice that we are less than fully alive but we have no puff left for the out-breath of our witness in the world.

We need to give ourselves permission to breathe in. There can be an anxiety among us that it is self-indulgent or irrelevant to give time to personal spiritual practice, especially when the world is in such a mess. We feel drawn to do what we can, in the time we have left, to mend it, and worry that prayer is a distraction from that. But, as early Friend William Penn knew, "...[t]rue godliness don't turn men out of the world but enables them to live better in it and excites their endeavours to mend it..."[1]

Spiritual practice throws open the doors of our hearts and lets the Light in. It is a continuing process of learning to connect with peace, light and love: "a daily choice to live out of the Great Self, not the small self".[2] This choice is both liberating and disconcerting, for our spiritual practice reveals what is alive in us, and what is not. It comforts, strengthens and brings joy. But it also takes us out of our comfort zone. It releases us from our illusions, sometimes slowly and gently, sometimes rudely and disturbingly. Early Friend Margaret Fell described how the Light will "rip you up, and lay you open".[3] That is not a comfortable experience, but it is necessary if we are to become truly human.

As this deep transformation takes place, throughout the rollercoaster ride, we are held in the Oneness from which we were born and in which we have our being: whether we experience highs or lows in our spiritual practice, at a deep level all is well.

As we persevere in our practice, we are likely to glimpse this truth more often. We may also draw strength from the testimony of others, be it the Buddha's teachings on finding happiness in the here and now, or mystic John of the Cross's poetry on divine love experienced in the "dark night of the soul". Early Friend Isaac Penington reassures and urges us:

> Give over thine own willing, give over thine own running,
> Give over thine own desiring to know or be anything,
> And sink down to the seed which God sows in thy heart
> and let that grow in thee and be in thee
> and breathe in thee and act in thee;
> and thou shalt find by sweet experience
> that the Lord knows that and loves and owns that,
> and will lead it to the inheritance of Life, which is its portion.

*Quaker faith & practice 26.70*

Our trouble is that we find it hard to let go. In our culture, we are surrounded by messages that we have to be someone, or save the world, or be successful in all our endeavours. We think that *simply being* is not enough. But we have to learn to let go and dare to simply be in the Presence, to experience our smallness and vulnerability. Then, and only then, can we begin to experience our true belonging, our essential belovedness, our oneness with all that is. That is the paradox of prayer.

## What is your experience of spiritual practice? How do you pray?

It does not matter *what* you do as spiritual practice, *how* you pray. It matters simply that you do it – in whatever way is right for you, right here, at this point in your life. American Friend Douglas Steere tells us:

> In prayer it is a matter of being present where we are…
> To pray is to pay attention to the deepest thing that we know…
> Prayer is the space in which we become truly human.

Sometimes Friends say "I've never heard prayer talked about among Quakers" or "I was never taught any of this spiritual practice stuff". Perhaps because modern liberal Friends lack shared words to speak of the mystery at the heart of life, we have become unsure of asking one another these questions, of speaking about spiritual practice or prayer. This makes sustaining ourselves as individuals and as a spiritual community challenging.

So this book of spiritual practices is offered to help Friends deepen the life of the Spirit, both as individuals and as a community. We hope that something here will speak to you in words or movements of the heart and body that are meaningful for you. We hope that something here will prove to be an opening for your own encounter with mystery, with love, with God.

## How do you make time?
## How do you establish a discipline of spiritual practice?

Once we have found a practice that speaks to us and made a start, there is no denying that it is a challenge to establish and maintain a regular discipline of spiritual practice amid all the hurly-burly of life. We do have something to help us, though: our essential human yearning for wholeness, for connection, for the Light. The Psalms speak of how:

> Like the deer that yearns
> for running streams,
> so my soul is yearning
> for you, my God.
> My soul is thirsting for God,
> the God of my life

*Psalm 42:2–3*

We long for release from our dream of separation. This gift is something that we can tune into, to help us when we feel distracted, unwilling or too busy to pursue our practice. Increasingly aware of that longing, we will find time for our practice, as we would for our most beloved friend. And we realise that it is not just the times we set aside for prayer, but that *anything* can become an opportunity for practice – pegging out the washing, travelling to work, eating a meal, waiting in a queue.

When we manage to establish some kind of habit of spiritual practice, however imperfect it is in our own eyes, we begin to open ourselves to the possibility of what St Paul called "prayer without ceasing". This does not mean that we mumble words of prayers as we go about our day, or spend hours in meditation. It simply means that we enable the Light to flood into our heart more easily at *any* time for having practised being open to that possibility. *This* is our communion, our daily spiritual bread. As Isaac Penington emphasised to early Friends, we must recognise the "necessity of depending on the Spirit for fresh light and life every day".[4]

# "We come to God through love, not navigation"
(St Augustine)

A collection of spiritual practices like this one risks suggesting that the practice itself matters, that more is better, or that we can pick and choose, moving on from one thing to another as the mood takes us.

We can get very hung up about methods, techniques in prayer. We cling on to them or repudiate them as if they were the point. But any spiritual practice is simply a doorway into the present moment, a gateway to Presence.

Experience teaches that it is better to find one practice that we feel drawn to, stay with it for a good length of time and not change it lightly. This allows the practice to benefit us with its own particular grace and to challenge us in its own particular way. It is only by staying with a practice beyond the point where we feel bored or inclined to try something else that we open ourselves to a deeper encounter with the divine; for this is the point at which we may have to let go of some of our usual attachments, notions or illusions.

Meister Eckhart warns that "whoever seeks God by ways is finding ways and losing God",[5] so hold your chosen practice lightly. When all is said and done, "all spiritual disciplines have one purpose: to get rid of illusions so that we can *be present*".[6]

To pray is to embark on a journey whose final destination is unknown to any of us. May the promptings of love and truth in your heart be your guide.

# Appleseed

Appleseed is a process that enables thinking and feeling to work together so that space can be made for the Spirit to be experienced and grow within. There are three stages in any Appleseed practice.

## Stage one: input

First of all there is some input related to the theme, which could be in words, prose or poetry, pictures or other visual material, or music. This input usually takes about half an hour at a led Appleseed event. You could experiment with different members of your worship group preparing the input for a group session, or you could use images, poetry or music from books, recordings or the internet.

## Stage two: response activities

The input is followed by a 'response activity', a very simple, arts-based exercise that gives time and space for colour and shapes to emerge and for new discoveries to be made. This stage lasts approximately three quarters of an hour.

Here are details of three different kinds of response activity. More response options are detailed in the Appleseed workbook (see *Find out more*).

### Spontaneous painting

This kind of painting is called 'spontaneous' to distinguish it from landscapes, still lifes or portraits, for example. The aim is to paint not what is 'out there' but what is 'in here'. You are invited to take an inward journey and to express it in colour, shape and texture.

1. Begin by wetting your paper on both sides, using a sponge.
2. Paint for one minute using both hands and with your eyes closed to enable you to let go and work in freedom.
3. Once the minute is up, open your eyes. You now have the opportunity to continue to develop your work in various ways, but there is no pressure to do so. For example, you could add further brush strokes or colours.

Note: It is best to use watercolour or gouache paints and good quality watercolour paper such as Bockingford.

## Word collage

This is an exercise in paying full attention to a word or phrase and exploring its meaning in a new way. You will make a collage composed entirely of letters and not of symbols or pictures. But you can interpret letter shapes very freely and arrange them in any order.

1. In the silence at the beginning, allow a word or short phrase, usually from the theme of the session, to come to mind.
2. Collect paper from a selection previously laid out; one sheet will be for your base paper, and others will be needed for your individual letters.
3. Tear the letters from any of the papers you have collected. Never use scissors, as they allow too much control. Tearing the paper involves both hands and releases creativity.
4. Do not glue the letters down until the end, as changes of mind about colours or arrangement often happen late in the process and can be very revealing.

## Postcards

Images are part of our everyday lives; they delight or frighten us, remind us or make us sad. But images can be precious learning points; they have been described as the language of the soul and can help us to discern where the Spirit is in our lives, and where we are being guided on our journey. By using a large number and great variety of postcards and photographs, it is possible to simulate the profusion of images we encounter in our lives and which flicker through our minds.

1. You begin this process by being given a word or concept that relates to the theme, for example my journey, my difficult place, my hope.
2. You then browse among the cards, letting one or two of them 'choose you'. There will be only ten minutes to do this, in order to encourage spontaneity.
3. After choosing there will be fifteen minutes to write about your cards. You can offer optional guidelines or queries to help people with this task.

# Stage three: worship sharing

This is an opportunity to share the experience of the response activity, or indeed the whole session, including the input. Worship sharing is used because it gives a protected space for participants to share as much, or as little, as they want; they draw their own parameters. They are protected from invasive questioning of their work, or what they say about it. Also important is that the process can take people into new discoveries about what their work is telling them.

# Find out more

- Cook, Chris and Brenda Heales. *Images and Silence: 1992 Swarthmore Lecture.* Quaker Books, 1992.
- Cook, Chris and Brenda Heales. *Seeding the Spirit: the Appleseed workbook.* Woodbrooke Quaker Study Centre, 2001.

# Bible study

## Setting up a Bible study group

The following are a few key points to bear in mind when setting up Bible study in your meeting or Quaker group:

- The ideal group size is relatively small (between four and eight people) so that all can contribute. It is important to have a settled group, so if other members of a meeting want to join once the group has started you should wait until a natural break in the study or establish another group.
- No previous study of the Bible is needed. Group members need not have ever picked up the Bible before to participate fully. A person with biblical knowledge can be helpful to the group but it is important that they do not take on leadership or are seen as an authority figure. A group reflecting a diversity of viewpoints provides a variety of spiritual experience and understanding.
- Share leadership of the group or rotate responsibility for facilitation amongst all members.

It is important to agree a fixed schedule for meetings.

- How often will you meet? Once a week or once a fortnight is preferable.
- How many weeks are you going to meet for? You could meet for several weeks in order to read one book of the Bible and then review whether you wish to continue.
- How long will each session last? An hour to an hour and a half for worship and study is usually sufficient.
- Where will you meet? The meeting house provides a neutral space. Meeting in people's homes makes a more intimate and relaxed atmosphere.

Consider whether you want to extend the experience by coming together for a shared meal before you do the Bible study. Doing this can give important time for fellowship and community building and strengthen the group.

## Studying the Bible: how to do it

Choose a book of the Bible that you are going to study – it is best not to skip around people's favourite passages, though you could choose to do this as an extra session at the end of the book. Study only a few verses each time. People should come having read the verses that you are going to study that session.

Having a variety of translations of the Bible can help the group to see that the authors/translators are human and that any one translation cannot reproduce all the meaning of the original text. There can be significant differences between one translation and another of the same text. Bible study in which members read from different translations makes the members more sensitive to the choice of words and the change in meaning when different words are used.

### Steps for each group session
1. Start with a short period of silence.
2. Read the passage aloud, sharing out the reading around the group.
3. Share your reflections. You may want to use some or all of the following as prompts:
   - What do you see as the key points in this passage?
   - What resonates with your experience in this passage?
   - What difficulties do you have with this passage?
   - What connections are there between this passage and Quaker beliefs and practices?
   - What occurred to you in reading this passage?
4. Finish with a short period of silence.

## Find out more

- Birkel, Michael L. *Engaging Scripture: reading the Bible with early Friends.* Friends United Press, 2005.
- Borg, Marcus. *Reading the Bible again for the first time: taking the Bible seriously but not literally.* HarperCollins, 2002.
- Buckley, Paul and Stephen W. Angell. *The Quaker Bible reader.* Earlham College Press, 2006.
- Spears, Larry and Joanne. *Friendly Bible Study.* Friends General Conference, 1990.
- Bible resources online at www.biblegateway.com
- Friendly Bible Study resources by Larry and Joanne Spears online at: www.read-the-bible.org/FriendlyBibleStudy.htm
- A lectionary online at: www.churchofengland.org/prayer-worship/worship/texts/common-worship-pdf-files.aspx
- A sacred texts archive online at: www.sacred-texts.com

# Body prayer

Praying with our bodies can be a powerful and simple way of opening to the divine reality. It helps us to bypass our busy, thinking minds, and connect with the Spirit at a deep level. As we repeat the movements, slowly, prayerfully, we may come to a depth of stillness in the midst of movement.

It is worth doing this practice for at least ten minutes to allow you to settle into that prayerful place in the body. Although it is usually done standing up, this practice can also be done while sitting down if you find it hard to stand for any length of time.

## Body prayer practice

1. **Gathering** Stand with your feet comfortably apart and hands held out in front of you. Slowly bring your hands together, gathering in all that you are, all that is loveable, wonderful, joyful, as well as the things that you would rather no one knew about – failures, disappointments and woundedness, bringing together all the elements that make up the unique individual whole.
2. **Focus** Bring your hands together, palm to palm at heart level. This signifies your intent to be present to God, your desire to offer consent to the promptings of love and truth within.
3. **Offering** With arms reaching up and hands open, reach out to express your longing and yearning for wholeness, for oneness with all that is.
4. **Receive** Lower your hands, palms up, to receive what this day offers – gifts, counsel, comfort, joy, awakening...
5. **Taking what is given** Cross your hands over your chest, taking these sacred gifts into yourself, feeling them throughout your whole body, absorbing them into your being.
6. **Offering yourself as a channel of gifts to the world** Lower your arms, palms facing forward to express your sharing of Life's gifts with others – loving service and ministry flowing through you.

*Adapted from* Being Fully Present to God *by Deborah Shaw*

# Find out more

- Pagitt & Prill. *Body Prayer*. WaterBrook Multnomah, 2006
- Roth, Nancy. *Spiritual Exercises: joining body and spirit in prayer*. Church Publishing Inc, 2005.
- Slosson Wuellner, Flora. *Prayer and Our Bodies*. Upper Room Books, 1987.
- 'Body and meditation' video link on 'Meditatio' channel main page at: www.youtube.com/user/meditatiowccm
- Introduction to body prayer at: http://storage.amazingdiscoveries.org/assets/ files/ADDownloads/References/RtR/PDF-909/Introduction%20to%20Body%20 Prayer.pdf
- Lord's Prayer body prayer video on You Tube at: www.youtube.com/watch?v=sxWOfNqobNY (or search Contemplative Fire – Body Prayer – The Lord's Prayer at: www.youtube.com)
- Mindful movements with Thich Nhat Hanh video on You Tube at: www.youtube.com/watch?v=oWerJwf3-3I (or search Thich Nhat Hanh – Mindful Movements at: www.youtube.com)

# Centering down practices

The breath is used widely and from ancient times in both Christian and Eastern prayer and meditation practices. There are many advantages of using the breath to centre down in Meeting for Worship or solitary prayer and meditation: you already know how to breathe; your breath is always with you; you don't need any equipment. It is free and always available.

Before we can make proper use of the breath, we must first accept it as a gift. We need to let it flow freely rather than try to control it. If we can simply relax totally and let go, we will find that our breathing, left to itself, will gradually slow down, deepen and become calm.

In each of the following exercises or aids to centering down, it is helpful to start by becoming aware of your body. Notice how you are sitting and try to sit in a relaxed but gently alert way. The flow of breath is helped by a good sitting posture and freedom from tension. Notice if there are any spots of tension in your body. One way of helping relieve the tension is to give it some attention and really tighten the tense muscles, keep them as tight as possible for a few seconds and then let the tension go. Another way is to breathe into the tension and gently release it. You might find that you need to come back to the spots of tension and repeat the tightening and releasing action as you begin the exercises.

In the West, we are taught from earliest youth to keep our stomachs in when we breathe. But, in these practices, allow your stomach to become soft and to expand as you breathe in. This takes in more air and deepens the breath. If it helps you, put your hand on your abdomen and feel it expand.

Each of the following exercises has been used over centuries. Each has variations but these are the basic forms.

## The first exercise: using the breath alone

In this exercise the simple act of counting helps focus the mind away from its usual busyness, while the breath helps both body and mind to become still.

1. Settle in the chair, perhaps acknowledging inwardly those around you when in Meeting for Worship.
2. Close your eyes or focus on a particular spot on the floor in front of you.
3. Take time to let your body relax. Notice any spots of tension. Be gentle – there is no rush and the calmer you are, the easier the breath will flow.

4. Become aware of your breathing – do not change it, just notice how you are breathing. Is your breathing shallow or deep? Is it fast or slow? Smooth or ragged? Just pay attention to taking in the life-giving air and releasing it.
5. Notice if the tension has returned and repeat the tension-relieving aid.
6. Gently, slowly, count up to five as you breathe in.
7. Hold that breath for a gentle count of five, the same length as the inward breath.
8. Release the breath and breathe out gently for the count of five.
9. Leave a space of a gentle count of five before taking in another breath and repeating the exercise from step 6.
10. Notice every so often if tension has crept in and gently relieve it in the same way as before.

## The second exercise: using a single word mantra with the breath

In this exercise the mantra helps to focus the mind. Without 'thinking' about the word and its meaning, a fuller sense of the word can come through the exercise of breathing.

Use the same method for starting as from steps 1 to 5 above.

6. As you gently breathe in, use a short one-syllable word. It could be the Eastern Om, a Christian word such as God or Lord, or a word like Life or Love. You may find that a word of your own comes to mind, or even just a single sound.
7. Gently breathe out and repeat the word or sound on the outward breath.
8. Notice every so often if tension has crept in and gently relieve it in the same way as before.
9. Keep breathing in and out using the mantra.

## The third exercise: using a short phrase mantra with the breath

In this exercise a phrase divided in two is recited on the incoming and outgoing breath. Again, it is the recitation of the phrase with the breath that can give a fuller meaning beyond the thought.

Use the same method for starting as from steps 1 to 5 above.

6. Choose a short phrase, or let a phrase come to you. It could be something like: 'Just being – here now'; 'Mara-natha' (Come Lord Jesus); 'Present moment – wonderful moment' or 'Into your hands – I commend my spirit'.
7. As you gently breathe in, recite the first part of the phrase or mantra (up to the dashes in the examples above).

8. As you breathe out recite the second half of the phrase or mantra.
9. Notice every so often if tension has crept in and gently relieve it in the same way as before.
10. Keep breathing in and out using the mantra.

Practising one of the above exercises for 10–30 minutes a day can make centering down in Meeting for Worship much easier.

There will be distractions and you will lose concentration from time to time – or many times – in the course of the time you have allowed yourself. Do not berate yourself for these distractions; be gentle with yourself and simply bring your focus back to your breathing each time.

## Find out more

- Freeman, Laurence. *Christian Meditation; your daily practice*. Novalis/Medio Media, 2001.
- Hughes OP, Louis. *Body-Mind Meditation: a gateway to spirituality*. The Mercier Press, 1990.
- Laird, Martin. *Into the Silent Lane: the practice of contemplation*. DLT, 2006.
- Main, John. *Word into Silence: a manual for Christian Meditation*. Canterbury Press, 2006.
- Main, John and Laurence Freeman. *The Heart of Creation: meditation – a way of setting God free in the world*. Canterbury Press, 2007.
- *The Big Silence*, a BBC television documentary about five people on a silent retreat, has some useful tips. See BBC website at: www.bbc.co.uk/programmes/b00vkk77
- Christian meditation guidance and talks on You Tube at: www.youtube.com/user/meditatiowccm
- Growing into Silence website offers details of retreats, resources and centres featured in *The Big Silence* programmes: http://growingintosilence.com
- The World Community for Christian Meditation website: www.wccm.org

# Centering Prayer: a practice of surrender

Centering Prayer is rooted in the Christian contemplative tradition. At the heart of the practice is the act of surrender to the loving power of the Divine. It is a practice not of attention or concentration but of 'letting go and letting God'. The prayer consists of an inner gesture of release, making space for the Spirit in our hearts.

The *intention* to be open to the work of divine love within is the key to Centering Prayer. A simple word (or the breath) is used as an anchor for our intention, but it is not a mantra to repeat or concentrate on; we simply return to it each time we realise that we have become distracted by a thought or sensation, as a way of re-focussing our intention to be open to the Spirit. If there are 10,000 distractions during our 20 minutes of practice, then we have 10,000 opportunities to re-open ourselves to the Spirit. That is the practice. It is not to achieve some kind of 'peaceful' non-thinking state but simply to make use of our thoughts as our way to practise letting go.

## Centering Prayer practice

1. Choose a sacred word as the symbol of your intention to surrender to the loving power of the Divine within.
   - It is best to use a short, simple word like God, Love, Listen, Peace, Let Go, Silence, Stillness, Trust, Jesus, Abba, Amma.
   - Instead of a sacred word, a simple inward glance toward the divine presence, or noticing one's breath may work better for some people.
   - The sacred word is sacred not because of its inherent meaning, but because of the meaning you give it as the expression of your intention to open yourself to the Divine and let go.
   - Having chosen a sacred word, it is best not to change it during the prayer period because that would simply be getting caught up in thoughts.

2. Find a well supported position that enables you to be comfortable but alert. With eyes gently closed, settle briefly and silently introduce the sacred word as the symbol of your consent to the divine presence and action within.
   - In Centering Prayer practice you can sit, kneel or lie down. It helps if your back is straight.

- Close your eyes as a symbol of letting go of what is going on around and within you.
- Introduce the sacred word inwardly as gently as laying a feather on your outstretched hand.
- If you fall asleep, simply continue the prayer as soon as you wake up. If you find yourself nodding off repeatedly, try opening your eyes and going to a gentle, soft focus instead.

3. When engaged with your thoughts, return ever-so-gently to the sacred word.
   - 'Thoughts' includes every perception, including body sensations, sense perceptions, feelings, images, memories, plans, reflections, concepts, commentaries, and spiritual experiences.
   - Thoughts are an inevitable, integral and normal part of Centering Prayer.
   - Use a minimum of effort when returning 'ever-so-gently' to the sacred word. This is the only activity you initiate during the time of Centering Prayer.
   - Each thought can be likened to a balloon, which you simply release as you become aware that you are holding it.
   - During the course of Centering Prayer, the sacred word may become vague or disappear.

4. At the end of the prayer period, remain in silence with eyes closed for a couple of minutes.

## Find out more

- Bourgeault, Cynthia. *Centering Prayer and Inner Awakening*. Cowley Publications, 2004.
- Keating, Thomas. *Open Mind, Open Heart*. Continuum, 2007.
- Pennington, M. Basil, Thomas Keating, Thomas E. Clarke. *Finding Grace at the Center: the beginning of Centering Prayer*. Skylight Paths Publishing, 2007 (3rd edition).
- Centering prayer guidelines at: www.youtube.com/watch?v=3IKpFHfNdnE (or search for Thomas Keating Centering Prayer guidelines intro at: www.youtube.com)
- Contemplative Outreach UK website: www.couk.org.uk
- Contemplative Outreach website introductory material: www.contemplativeoutreach.org/getting-started

# Experiment with Light

Experiment with Light is a spiritual practice used by Friends as a way of opening to the Light in relation to specific aspects of their lives. Experiment with Light attempts to recover the practice of early Friends so that modern people can discover for themselves 'the power of the Light' to enlighten and transform their lives. This practice can open us to a truth that reveals more deeply who we are, what we can trust and believe in, and how we can live our lives more freely and fully.

There are forms of the Experiment with Light practice for individuals and groups, but, for many people, the Light meditation is best practised within a group of Friends who can provide each other with emotional support when needed. As with any spiritual practice, the Light meditation may trigger insights that can be challenging as well as comforting.

The modern Experiment with Light practice has adapted early Friends' practice of 'waiting in the Light' to our present needs and understandings, involving a simple meditative process in four stages.

## A simple Experiment with Light practice

The Light meditation can be separated into four main steps, with an invitation first to be still:

1. Find a well supported position that enables you to be comfortable but alert. Let any tension go from your body and take a moment to settle into stillness. Allow yourself to be open and receptive.
2. **Mind the light** Gently, gradually, allow yourself to become aware of what is going on in your life, what the real concerns are, where there is any discomfort or uncertainty. You may wish to focus on specific areas of your life.
3. **Open your heart to the truth** Spend some time simply letting the Light reveal to you what is really going on, what makes you feel as you do about this issue. Keep a little distance rather than becoming tangled up in the issue itself. Do not look for answers or focus on any confusion, discomfort or hurt, but on the Light that reveals it. Look closely at what is going on as it is being disclosed to you by the Light.

4.  **Wait in the Light** Do not turn away until you have seen the whole picture, or as much as is right for you just now. This waiting in the Light can sometimes be enlightening and liberating. When clarity comes or an answer is revealed, you will recognise its truth, however unexpected or even uncomfortable. If you do not reach clarity during this period of practice, do not worry. The Light may reveal truth to us gradually as we are able to process and accept it.

5.  **Submit to the truth** Say yes to whatever truth has been revealed to you. Accept fully what has been disclosed of the reality of your life. This acceptance brings peace of mind and helps you to live in accordance with this new insight.

6.  When you are ready, bring your meditation to a close.

## Find out more

*   Experiment with Light talks and meditation guides are available on audio tape and CD from the Quaker Centre at Friends House. There are Light Groups in many areas where Friends can practise the meditation together.
*   Ambler, Rex. *Light to Live by: an exploration in Quaker spirituality*. Quaker Books, 2008 (2nd edition).
*   Ambler, Rex. *Truth of the Heart: an anthology of George Fox*. Quaker Books, 2007 (2nd edition).
*   Barbour, Hugh & J. William Frost. *The Quakers*. Friends United Press, 1988.
*   Lampen, John. *Seeing, Hearing, Knowing: reflections on Experiment with Light*. Sessions, 2008.
*   Experiment with Light website for meditation guides, news of upcoming events and courses, newsletters: www.experiment-with-light.org.uk

# Gratitude practices

Practices of gratitude and thanksgiving are found in all spiritual traditions. They help us deepen our awareness of our connection with all that is and of our inter-dependence with the world and other people. Practising gratitude for all the ordinary everyday blessings of our lives can lead to a peaceful heart and a simpler, more sustainable way of life.

## Three treasures practice

1. At some point today, take time out to notice three 'treasures' from the day for which you are grateful.
2. These could be big things or tiny things: a hug from a friend, a wonderful film, an achievement at work or school, a tasty dinner, some good news.
3. They could be things that we do not even notice usually: eyes that work, a fridge with food in, being able to walk safely to the shops, someone's company.
4. Find a way of recording or sharing these treasures. You could write them down in a journal, draw them on a poster, put a sticky note on your fridge door, tell your partner just before you go to sleep, email/text/tweet about them to friends.
5. Try doing this practice every day for a month and see how it affects your sense of connectedness with the world and others.

## Web of life meditation

1. Select an everyday object and sit quietly with it. It could be anything from a dish of food to a bunch of keys, a toy, a piece of art, a brick, a sock. You can hold it or place it somewhere nearby where you can see it clearly.
2. Take your time to become aware of the shape, colour, feel, texture, sound, smell and even taste of the object.
3. Become aware of its parts, wonder what each is made from, how each part was made, where and by whom. Reflect with gratitude on each person and natural force involved in the origin of the object.
4. Again, taking your time, allow your awareness to spread to include how the object came to you, where it travelled, who handled or brought it. This could include natural forces, human labour and preparation, transport, packaging, selling, giving and receiving.

5.  If you wish, you can extend this to include the future of the object – who will hold or use it after you, how it may be disposed of or recycled.
6.  As you become aware of each person in this web of connection, hold them in the Light, with all their hopes and fears, their joys, loves and struggles.
7.  Finally, spend some time once more simply being with the object. Allow a feeling of gratitude to arise in connection with whatever has spoken to you in this practice today.

## Find out more

- Pradervand, Pierre. *The Gentle Art of Blessing*. Cygnus Books, 2010.
- Steindl-Rast, David. *Gratefulness, the Heart of Prayer: an approach to life in fullness*. Paulist Press, 1998.
- How to Start a Gratitude Practice to Change Your Life, online at: http://tinybuddha.com/blog/how-to-start-a-gratitude-practice-to-change-your-life
- The Transformative Power of Gratitude article at: www.beliefnet.com/Wellness/Gratitude/The-Transformative-Power-Of-Gratitude

# Journalling as spiritual practice

Journalling is a way of using writing to explore events, relationships, attitudes, feelings or reflections in such a way as to illuminate their meaning for us. It is a form of writing that is entirely for our own personal use, and not for any external audience. In particular, journalling provides a creative way of exploring our spiritual life. Spiritual journalling is different from keeping a diary. The process of journalling allows for reflection, discovery, insight, new thoughts and feelings, opening to the Spirit, or revisiting and resolving past episodes. It can also provide a new way of engaging with more traditional categories of prayer and the spiritual life: self-examination, intercession, meditation, praise, petition, confession, and so on.

Some people write in their journals when the need or mood takes them. Others use daily writing as a form of spiritual discipline, for example reflecting at the end of each day on queries such as: What of today can I give thanks for? How has the Spirit been at work in/through me today? Have I shown God's face to the world in how I have lived today?

## Privacy

We all have a great ability to deceive ourselves, to gloss over our actions and responses, to be selective or economical with the truth. Privacy in journal writing removes the external audience for whom we might (consciously or unconsciously) shape our reflections. We still have our own inner audience to contend with – how truthful are we being with ourselves?

Writing a journal for one's own spiritual growth and discipline is most effective when kept utterly private – no playing to the gallery, no censoring, no subtle shifts of emphasis. We can write spontaneously and without artifice.

## Tools

Writing on paper with a pen or pencil is a different experience from writing at a keyboard. The former is more immediate, has more contact with emotions and memories, because that is how we first learned to write. In general, this is the approach recommended for journalling, unless there are overriding reasons to use a keyboard.

If this is new for you, you will need a book to write in – it is probably better not to use loose-leaf paper but a book, so that you are not tempted to throw pages away. A4 is a good size for a more expansive feel. Most stationers carry a range of attractive hard-bound notebooks – choose something that appeals to your eye, that will draw you into it.

If you think you might want to draw or paint, as well as write, then choose a book with plain, unlined pages. Always use a pen or pencil that is comfortable in your hand and does not cause physical strain. And feel free to experiment with felt pens and coloured inks to express what you want to set on the page.

# Find out more

## How-to books

- Adams, Kathleen. *Journal to the Self: twenty-two paths to personal growth*. Grand Central Publishing, 1990.
- Baldwin, Christian. *Life's Companion: journal writing as spiritual quest*. Bantam, 1990.
- Klassen, Joanne. *Tools of transformation: write your way to new worlds of possibility – in just 5 minutes*. Infinity Publishing, 2004.
- Peace, Richard. *Spiritual Journaling: recording your journey towards God*, NavPress, 1998.
- Rainer, Tristine. *The New Diary: how to use a journal for self-guidance and expanded creativity*. Distributed by St. Martin's Press; Some Highlighting edition, 1978.

## Related reading

- Leonard, Alison *Telling Our Stories, wrestling with a fresh language for the spiritual journey*. DLT, 1995.
- Morrison, Mary. *The Journal and the Journey* (Pendle Hill Pamphlet 242). Pendle Hill, 1982.
- Skidmore, Gil. *Turning Inside Out: an exploration of spiritual autobiography*. The Sowle Press, 1996.
- *Sharing our journeys: excerpts from the Philadelphia Yearly Meeting Quaker Studies Program on journal writing, spiritual friendship and group conversation*. Quaker Resources for Learning, Quaker Home Service and Woodbrooke, 1995.

# Listening prayer

Listening lies at the heart of the Quaker way. This listening prayer practice is simple but challenges us to listen deeply both to ourselves and to another. There is no discussion, only listening. Listening deeply and prayerfully to one another can draw both speaker and listener to a deeper understanding of the sacred thread running through their lives.

## Listening prayer practice

1. Find a partner to do the listening prayer practice with you and a quiet place where you will not be interrupted.
2. Each of you will have five minutes to speak while the other person listens without interrupting. Your speaking and listening time will be surrounded by time when both of you will be silent together.
3. Agree which of you will speak first and then agree a focus question, such as 'In what ways have you experienced God in your life during the last week?' or 'What has been going on in your prayer life this month?'
4. Begin the practice with five minutes of shared silence to enable you both to become still and centered.
5. The first person then has five minutes to speak without interruption (and afterwards there should be no commentary on what is said). The first listener keeps time and signals the beginning and end of the five minutes.
6. There is then a five-minute silence for centering before the second person speaks.
7. The second person speaks for five minutes.
8. Finish with another five minutes of shared, prayerful silence.

## Find out more

- Edwards, Tilden H. *Spiritual Friend*. Paulist Press, 1980.
- Guenther, Margaret. *Holy listening: the art of spiritual direction*. DLT, 1992.
- Leech, Kenneth. *Soul friend: spiritual direction in the modern world*. DLT, 1994.
- Long, Ann. *Listening*. DLT, 1990.
- O'Donohue, John. *Anam Cara*. Bantam, 1999.
- Roberts, Trish. *More than equals: spiritual friendships*. Pendle Hill, 1999 (Pendle Hill Pamphlet 345).

- Wall, Ginny. *Becoming Friends: preparing to be a companion: handbook.* Quaker Books, 2010.
- *Sharing our journeys: excerpts from the Philadelphia Yearly Meeting Quaker Studies Program on journal writing, spiritual friendship and group conversation.* Quaker Resources for Learning, Quaker Home Service and Woodbrooke, 1995.
- *This is who I am: listening with older Friends.* Committee on Eldership and Oversight, Quaker Books, 2003.

# Mindfulness of breath

Mindfulness is a practice of awareness based in the Buddhist tradition. It involves stopping and being present to what is, cultivating a deep and focussed attention to the here and now. This helps us to let go of our usual anxious clinging to thoughts of the past or fantasies about the future, and to accept with a clear mind and a compassionate heart life as it really is, ourselves as we really are, right here right now.

Mindfulness practices are very simple, but not necessarily easy! We get distracted. We think the idea is to practise until we are free of thoughts or distractions. But this is a misconception. Mindfulness practice simply involves returning to our focus each time we get distracted, without judgement. Little by little, we let go of seeking results or a special experience and find that we are waking up to who we truly are.

Practising mindful awareness of our breath can offer, in its simplicity, a profound experience of connecting with the sacred in the present moment.

## Mindfulness of breath practice

1. Begin by taking a moment to check your posture. You can, of course, do breathing practice in any position, but it can be very helpful to sit in a well-supported upright position: whatever position you choose, the important thing is to find one that enables you to be both relaxed and alert.
2. You may find it helpful to close your eyes gently.
3. Take a moment to release any tightness from your muscles – you can do this by imagining tension simply flowing away on each out-breath for several breaths. Don't forget areas that are often quite tense, such as shoulders, back and face.
4. Now bring your focus to your breathing. Simply let your attention rest on your breath, allowing it to flow naturally. Follow your breath with your full attention as it flows in and out of your body.
5. As you watch, notice how each breath is different: sometimes shallow, sometimes deep; smooth or ragged; fast or slow; cool or warm; silent or with a sound.
6. You may like to focus your awareness in one place as you watch your breath: the rise and fall of your chest or abdomen, or the feeling of air passing at the back of your throat or through your nose.
7. Continue to watch your breath with mindful attention for the rest of the time you have set aside.

8. Each time distractions arise, just bring your attention back to your breath, gently and without judgement. There's no success or failure. Just breathing. Simply being present to what is.

## Find out more

- There is a mindfulness of sound practice in the Sound and Light section of this book on page 31.
- Brown, Valerie. *Living from the Centre: mindfulness meditation and centering for Friends* (Pendle Hill Pamphlet 407). Pendle Hill, 2010.
- Thich Nhat Hanh. *The Miracle of Mindfulness: the classic guide to meditation by the world's most revered master*. Rider, 2008.
- Thich Nhat Hanh. *Peace Is Every Step: the path of mindfulness in everyday life*. Rider, 1991.
- Kabat-Zinn, Jon. *Full Catastrophe Living: how to cope with stress, pain and illness using mindfulness meditation*. Piatkus Books, 2001.
- Kabat-Zinn, Jon. *Wherever You Go, There You Are: mindfulness meditation for everyday life*. Piatkus Books, 2004.
- Kornfield, Jack. *A Path with Heart*. Rider, 2002.
- Kornfield, Jack. *Meditation For Beginners*. Bantam, 2005.
- Manning, Tara Jon. *Mindful knitting: inviting contemplative practice to the craft*. Tuttle Publications, 2004.
- Community of Interbeing, UK community who follow the teachings of Thich Nhat Hanh, website at: http://interbeing.org.uk
- Mindfulness meditation (video guidance) on You Tube at: www.youtube.com/watch?v=a_xEGLueiLM
- Mindful UK website giving information about mindfulness resources and events in the UK, at: www.mindfuluk.org.uk
- Plum Village website, Thich Nhat Hanh's monastic community, with information about mindfulness at: www.plumvillage.org/mindfulness-practice

# A review of the day

Reflecting on the events of each day can help us see the work of the Spirit in our lives – the sacred in the everyday. It is a central part of the Ignatian spiritual tradition, where it is known as an 'examen' or examination of consciousness.

Like beachcombing, the review of the day practice can help you notice all kinds of things that you may have passed over in the busyness of the day. As you prayerfully explore the mystery of yourself in the midst of your daily actions, you can grow more familiar with your own spirit and become more aware of the promptings of Love and Truth within you.

## Review of the day practice

1. Begin by taking a moment to still yourself and become open to the presence of God/the Spirit.
2. Accept and be thankful for any gifts that the day has brought, however small – a smile or kindness, work done, a glimpse of beauty, even the resilience that has enabled you to get to the end of the day in one piece!
3. Let the Light of the Spirit shine on the events of your day and on your own actions, attitudes and motives, helping you to be open to growth.
4. Now go over the events of the day briefly in your mind, from the moment you woke up until the present moment.
   With each event, observe not just what happened but also your thoughts, feelings and responses. Do not judge yourself or the event – just observe.
5. Are there any things in the experience of your day today, however small or seemingly insignificant, that you notice, that particularly catch your attention? Be still and allow yourself to be with whatever surfaces in connection with each experience.
6. Open yourself to any new ways of seeing or understanding that may arise.
   Are there ways you responded to or cooperated with the promptings of Love and Truth in your heart? Are there ways you resisted them?
   Are there ways in which you feel God is calling you to a change of heart? Or to a new response to pain or joy in your life?
7. Let yourself really see deeply, allowing the Light to shine on the experiences of your day, speaking to your heart, challenging, encouraging and teaching you.
8. Open your heart to the grace to respond to what has come up.

# Find out more

- Campbell-Johnson, Michael. *Time To Change: An Ignatian retreat in everyday life*. DLT, 2010.
- Ignatian Spirituality website, with information, resources and links about the 'daily examen' at: http://ignatianspirituality.com/ignatian-prayer/the-examen
- Jesuit Retreats and Spirituality Centres website, with information about retreats and events based in Ignatian spirituality at: www.beunos.com/jesuitretreats
- Pray-as-you-go website, with audio download of review of the day prayer at: www.pray-as-you-go.org
- A Network for Grateful Living website at www.gratefulness.org

# Sacred reading (lectio divina)

Sacred reading has been part of the Christian prayer tradition for centuries and is an important spiritual practice for many people today. It is different from our normal, analytical reading of information and involves a slow meditative reading of a short text – reading not so much with the mind as with the heart. Sacred reading is a practice that invites us to make a contemplative journey into the heart of scripture and other texts, where we can meet the Spirit at work right here and now.

We are used to reading for information, scanning swiftly and analytically, using our mind to reach an understanding of a text's content. Or perhaps we are a reader of novels and blogs, where we read with a desire to get to the end of the page, chapter or book in order to find out what happens next to the characters, or who is enmeshed in scandal in the news.

Sacred reading is completely different from these kinds of approaches. It is reading for the heart. It does not ignore our mind, however. The combination of the text's content to stir both heart and mind, together with our intention to be open to grace, allows an integration of the experience of our heart and our cognitive understanding, which goes against our cultural trends.

> From this time forward
> I make you hear new things
> Hidden things that you have not known.
> They are created now, not long ago;
> Before today you have never heard of them,
> So that you could not say,
> "I already knew them."
>
> *(Isaiah 48:6–7)*

## Sacred reading practice

1. Begin by choosing a short extract from a sacred text: this could be the Bible, poetry, other sacred writings or anything that speaks deeply to you.
   Even this choosing can be done in a way that allows the text to 'choose' you, rather than you making an intellectual selection; for example, you could choose at random from a collection of extracts or use a lectionary or book of daily readings.

2. Read the text slowly and meditatively two or three times. Allow the words to soak in.

3. Is there a word or phrase that jumps out at you?
   Allow yourself to become aware of any words that cause a particular response, whether because they speak deeply and positively to you or perhaps cause resistance in you.

4. Now read the passage again, lingering over this word or phrase. Pay attention to what resonates in you, to your own response to the words. Stay with the word or phrase and repeat or reread them as often as you wish.
   It can be helpful to spend 10 or 15 minutes simply meditating on the word or phrase by repeating it (aloud or silently) in this way.

5. Allow the words to speak to you at a deep level. What is the Spirit teaching you through this word or phrase and your response to it?

6. If you feel drawn to make any kind of response to this deep reflection, give expression to it: this could be in prayer, writing, drawing, or simply speaking to God about it.

7. Then spend some time in silent waiting on God – not necessarily expecting an answer to any questions, but simply resting in contemplation of the divine presence in your heart.

8. As you move back into the ordinary activities of your day, do you feel called to live out any understanding you have reached as a result of this practice of sacred reading?

## Find out more

- Brueggemann, Walter. *Praying the Psalms*. St Mary's Press, 1982.
- Casey, Michael. *Sacred Reading: the ancient art of lectio divina*. Liguori Publications, 1996.
- Hall, Thelma. *Too deep for words: rediscovering Lectio Divina; with 500 Scripture texts for prayer*. Paulist Press, 1988.
- Kelly, Carole Marie. *A Handful of Fire: praying contemplatively with Scripture*. Twenty-third Publications, 2001.
- Sacred reading practice (by its traditional name of lectio divina) introduction and article on the Sisters of Saint Clare website at:
  http://srsclare.com/practice-of-prayer/lectio-divina
  http://srsclare.com/practice-of-prayer/lectio-divina/lectio-divina-fr-luke

# Sound and Light: healing relationships with the world and others

> When someone asks us where we want to be in our lives, the last thing
> that occurs to us is to look down at our feet and say, 'Here, I guess, since
> this is where I am.'

*Barbara Taylor Bradford*

So often we are not 'at one' with the world or people around us. We spend time and energy resisting the circumstances we find ourselves in or the people we are given to make community with, rather than responding creatively or with compassion. Here are two practices that can help heal us and the way we relate to the world and others.

## A mindfulness practice using sounds

This deceptively simple practice reaches deep into our capacity for judgement and separation, gently releasing us from our resistance to 'what is'. We discover that we tend to judge some sounds as 'good' and others as 'bad', when they are simply vibrations in the air: we react very differently to birdsong or the gurgling laugh of a baby compared to power tool noises or our stomach rumbling loudly in Meeting for Worship!

But all sounds are simply part of 'what is'. We can practise suspending our normal judgements and simply resting in the 'ocean' of being. In this way, *any* sound becomes a blessing, a simple invitation to return to the Eternal Now. This is a particularly useful practice to turn to when sounds are irritating us, or in everyday situations like waiting for a train or bus.

1. Begin by taking a moment to become aware of your body and its surroundings. Take a moment to release any tightness from your muscles – you can do this by imagining tension simply flowing away on each out-breath for several breaths.
2. You may find it helpful to close your eyes gently, depending on where you are.
3. Now bring your focus to the sounds around you. Simply listen to them – the loud ones and the soft, the distant and the near. Listen as if you were hearing sounds for the first time.

4. For the period of your practice, let your attention rest on each sound as it comes into your awareness, then let it go, noticing how each sound passes. Allow all sounds simply to *be* in your awareness, like clouds passing in a blue sky.
   - You may notice that what at first seems to be just one sound may be a combination of many sounds. Now listen to all those sounds not as separate entities but as making, all together, one vast symphony that fills the entire universe.
   - You may discover "a deep silence in the heart of all sounds".[7]

## A 'holding in the Light' practice

Hold yourself and others in the Light,
knowing that all are cherished by God.

*Advices & queries 3*

This practice focuses first on ourselves, next on someone whom we know only a little or feel neutral about, then on someone whom we find it harder to warm to. (It may be best not to focus on someone we have strong negative feelings about when we are new to this practice, but the practice can bring real healing here too.) While similar to Buddhist loving-kindness meditations, this practice follows a deeply Quaker approach: we practise holding in the Light as a way of 'letting go and letting God' into our relationships – both with ourselves and those around us.

1. Begin by taking a moment to check your posture and release any tension from your body – you can do this by imagining tension simply flowing away on each out-breath for several breaths.
2. Now bring your focus to yourself. Feel the floor under your feet, the chair holding you up ... and allow yourself to simply *rest* in the Light. You do not have to do anything. Simply be. If you find it helpful, you may imagine this Light bathing you like warm, gentle spring sunshine.
3. You may like to use some very simple phrases to focus your upholding of yourself; these can be repeated silently or under your breath throughout your period of prayer. Phrases could include one or two like the following:

   may I be well
   may I be free from suffering
   may I be happy
   may I be at peace

bless me in my sleeping
bless me in my waking
bless me in my good moods
bless me in my bad moods

bless me when I...

4.  Do not hurry this first stage of the practice. Allow yourself to experience the comfort or the challenge of holding yourself in the Light.
5.  When you feel ready, move your focus to someone whom you know only a little or feel neutral about, for example someone you have met briefly in a shop.
6.  Now hold this person in the Light, allowing the divine energy to gently enfold them. If it helps, you could repeat one or two of the phrases above to focus your intention, for example "may you be well" or "bless you in your sleeping/working etc."
7.  Again, do not hurry this stage of the practice. Allow yourself to be aware of the miracle of this person's life as you hold them in the Light. You may feel nothing; that is fine – simply let go and allow God's compassion to take over. Or you may find yourself wondering what this person's joys and sorrows are, or feeling a sense of connection and compassion towards them. Either is fine.
8.  When you are ready, move on to the final stage of bringing into your awareness a person whom you find it harder to warm to. Repeat steps 6 and 7 in relation to this person.
9.  You may like to end this practice with a brief period of silence, a spoken prayer or a few gentle breaths.

## Find out more

- There is a mindfulness of breath practice in this book on page 25 and further reading and links relating to mindfulness practices.
- de Mello, Anthony. *Sadhana: a way to God – Christian exercises in eastern form.* Bantam Doubleday Dell, 1978.
- O'Donohue, John. *An Abundance of Blessings: 52 meditations to illuminate your life.* Potter Style, 2012.
- O'Donohue, John. *Benedictus: a book of blessings.* Bantam, 2007.
- Pradervand, Pierre. *The Gentle Art of Blessing.* Cygnus Books, 2010.
- Loving-kindness meditation guidance (based on the Buddhist approach) on Mindfulnet website at: www.mindfulnet.org/Loving%20Kindness%20Practice.pdf and on Buddhanet website at: www.buddhanet.net/metta_in.htm

# Spiritual friendship/ companionship groups

## Why have a group?

As a community with no set-aside ministry we need to look to one another for spiritual learning and growth.

Spiritual friendship groups can be set up in meetings to help Friends know each other in the things that are eternal, as well as in the everyday. They are useful in large meetings to help anchor people, and in smaller meetings they help Friends to focus beyond practical tasks.

They enable Friends to offer each other a deep level of trust, mutual support, and sometimes challenge too.

## Ways to set up a group

Elders have responsibility for the spiritual life of the meeting so they will be involved in agreeing the setting up of a meeting-based group or groups. It can be helpful to have a few people organising the groups if there is more than one – this does not have to be an Elder.

Groups of between three and six people are about right, and meeting every four to six weeks seems to work well. It helps to agree where the groups will meet. It is nice if this can work in people's homes, but sometimes because of accessibility or public transport needs groups might be held in the meeting's premises.

Ways of eliciting interest include a meeting's newsletter, meeting notice board (with a sign-up sheet), talking with people, or making use of notices after Meeting for Worship. It helps to be clear who the contact person is.

## Ways of running a group

It can be helpful to agree the 'ground rules', for example:
- agreeing levels of confidentiality;
- deciding how long each gathering will last;
- exploring the balance between social/chat time and focussed spiritual time;
- ensuring everyone is heard and gets the chance to speak;

- deciding whether or not there will be food (and noting any dietary needs);
- agreeing if it is a closed group (and, if so, whether this is a permanent situation);
- establishing the level of commitment required;
- leading – one person, in turn, for how many sessions etc;
- identifying how topics are decided;
- deciding if there will be between-meetings 'work' to do (e.g. reading, following a spiritual practice etc);
- making contact if someone cannot come.

# Some examples of group activities

## Processes
- Journalling
- Sharing our stories
- Mapping understandings, journeys, connections
- Sharing music, poetry, art or prose
- Reflecting on natural objects
- Sacred reading
- Bible study
- Co-operative creative activities
- Plasticine ministry*
- Devising advices and queries
- Worship sharing

## Topics
- Our spiritual journeys
- Spiritual challenges
- Ways of talking about the Divine
- End of life
- Significant life events
- Festivals and seasons
- Testimony
- Discernment
- Resolutions

*Plasticine ministry*: Each person has a small piece of plasticine, which they shape during a period of silent worship, usually in response to a theme. Then follows worship sharing when each person can speak to what they have created, or allow it to speak for itself. The activity closes with further waiting worship.

# Find out more

- Clement, Daphne. *Group spiritual nurture: the wisdom of spiritual listening.* Pendle Hill, 2004 (Pendle Hill Pamphlet 373).
- Farnham, Suzanne, Stephanie Hull & R. Taylor McLean. *Grounded in God: listening hearts discernment for group deliberations.* Morehouse Publications, 1999.
- Leonard, Alison. *Telling our stories: wrestling with a fresh language for the spiritual journey.* DLT, 1995.
- O'Donohue, John. *Anam Cara.* Bantam, 1999.
- Pranis, Kay. *The Little Book of Circle Processes.* Good Books, 2005.
- Priestman, Rosalind. *Listening to one another: some ideas about creative listening groups and other ways of getting to know one another.* Woodbrooke, 1999.
- Roberts, Trish. *More than equals: spiritual friendships.* Pendle Hill, 1999 (Pendle Hill Pamphlet 345).
- Wheatley, Margaret. *Turning to one another: simple conversations to restore hope to the future.* Berrett-Koehler Publishers, 2002.
- *Sharing our journeys: excerpts from the Philadelphia Yearly Meeting Quaker Studies Program on journal writing, spiritual friendship and group conversation.* Quaker Resources for Learning. Quaker Home Service, and Woodbrooke, 1995.

# Visualisation – imaginative prayer

Visualisation is a form of spiritual practice that uses our imagination as a gateway to communion with our deepest self, with God. It is a practice found in traditions in both East and West. It is particularly important in the Ignatian tradition of Christian spirituality: Ignatius "uses pictures and images to present what is otherwise beyond all conceiving".[8] Using our imagination can help us get beyond what we think we *ought* to feel or experience in prayer and free us to become more aware of our real deep desires and the leadings of the Spirit. Imaginative prayer seeks the truth of the heart.

Some people find imaginative prayer difficult. They may not be able to picture the scene easily, yet they may have some intuition or gut reaction to the story or setting. Or they may hear or feel the story or place more than visualise it. Pray as you are able and be open to whatever comes.

Here are two very different kinds of visualisation practice that you may like to try.

## Imaginative prayer in the Ignatian tradition

1.  Choose a passage from Scripture to work with. Imaginative prayer works well with any scene from the Gospel or Old Testament where there is action taking place; it is not suited to passages of teaching or poetry. You could try:

    | | |
    |---|---|
    | Matthew 14:22–33 | Peter walks on the water |
    | Mark 10:46–52 | The cure of Bartimaeus |
    | Luke 5:1–11 | Call of four disciples |
    | John 4:1–42 | Jesus meets a woman at the well |
    | John 13:1–17 | Jesus washes the disciples' feet |
    | Exodus 3:1–6 | Moses and the burning bush |
    | 1 Samuel 3:1–10 | The call of Samuel. |

2.  Find a comfortable position and take a moment to become still and quiet.

3. Open yourself to the Spirit working through your imagination as you pray with the passage. You may want to focus this intention through a few words of prayer, for example expressing your hope for an encounter with Love, Truth, Jesus; or you may prefer to simply spend a moment in expectant and open listening.
4. Now read through the text a few times until you are thoroughly familiar with the story.
5. Let the scene build up in your mind's eye. Take your time. Use all your senses, seeing what is around you, hearing the sounds of the place, feeling, smelling, tasting. Lose yourself in the story. You may find this easier with your eyes shut.
6. Where are you in the scene? Take your own place in the scene as it unfolds. You may find that you are a bystander, a named person in the story, one of the central characters, or simply entering the action as yourself.
7. Allow yourself to be drawn into conversation with Jesus or another participant. Say whatever you want to, and give the one to whom you are speaking a chance to respond. Let the conversation continue as long as one of you has something to say. You may find that you move back and forth between the conversation and silently observing the scene several times during your prayer.
8. Stay in the scene for as long as the period you have set aside. Then draw your prayer to a close.
9. Afterwards, take some time to reflect on the experience. What struck you? What did you feel or desire? What will you take with you from this experience? Is there any part of this scene that you might want to revisit at another time?

## A sky meditation

1. Find a comfortable position and take a moment to become still and quiet. Pay attention to your breath for a few breaths to help you become centered.
2. Now picture a clear sky, in day or night time. You may find this easier with your eyes shut. Take your time. Be aware of the colour of the sky, the sense of depth, the quality of the light, the sense of boundlessness.
3. As you watch the sky, allow thoughts that arise in your mind to pass like clouds, light and insubstantial, through the vast stillness of the sky. Simply notice the shapes and colours of the clouds, allowing them to pass overhead, while the sky remains vast, deep, still.
4. If insistent thoughts, plans, feelings come, you could picture them as birds flying overhead, like loudly honking geese crossing the sky. Rather than trying to chase them away – to no avail – stop and look up. Allow yourself to experience and be one with the moving birds, see the beauty of their repeating patterns against the sky, their repeating sound. Simply watch and let the birds be. Let them pass.

5. After a while, the sky may become quieter. Bring your attention back to the colour of the sky, the sense of depth, the quality of the light, the sense of boundlessness.
6. More clouds may come. More birds may come. Just watch them come and let them go. Simply be there, one with the sky, which does not change as the clouds and birds pass through.
7. When your practice time is up, gently bring your attention back to your breath for a few breaths, then bring the practice to a close.

# Find out more

## Ignatian imaginative contemplation
- de Mello, Anthony. *Sadhana, a Way to God*. Doubleday, 1978.
- de Mello, Anthony. *Wellsprings: a book of spiritual exercises*. Doubleday, 1984.
- Hughes, Gerard W. *God of Surprises*. DLT, 1985.
- Silf, Margaret. *Landmarks: exploration of Ignatian spirituality*. DLT, 1998.
- Walker, Andrew. *On Retreat: a Lenten journey*. Continuum, 2012.
- 'Praying with our imaginations' page on Jesuit Creighton university website at: http://onlineministries.creighton.edu/CollaborativeMinistry/Imagination
- Ignatian spirituality website, with articles and links on Ignatian imaginative prayer, at: http://ignatianspirituality.com/ignatian-prayer/the-spiritual-exercises/ignatian-contemplation-imaginative-prayer

## Nature and Buddhist visualisation
- Kabat-Zinn, Jon. *Wherever You Go, There You Are*. Hearst Publications, 1994 (includes mountain meditation practice).
- Kornfield, Jack. *The Wise Heart: a guide to the universal teachings of Buddhist psychology*. Bantam, 2008 (includes visualisation practice).
- Mountain meditation practice at: http://thistimethisspace.com/2010/01/07/meditation-practice-mountain-meditation-for-beginners

# Walking meditation

## Our bodies as instruments of devotion

Taking our worship for a walk can be like a bridge linking the stillness of Meeting for Worship with the activity of our lives in the world. Meditating on one or two words while we walk may help to quiet the mind and prepare us for fuller opening to the Spirit. This walking meditation can be done before or after a period of worship, offering a transitional activity for deepening and engagement.

## Walking meditation practice

1. Read aloud a short inspirational text, which may be a poem, a brief passage from *Quaker faith & practice*, *Advices & queries* or some other writing. It is advisable to read it once at a normal steady speed and a second time much more slowly, with pauses between phrases.
2. Allow just two words from the text to stay with you. Let the other words fall away and simply focus on the two words that have particularly spoken to you.
3. Begin to walk quite slowly in a clockwise direction, making a circle around the room/space. Allow your body and arms to sway naturally. Keep your shoulders relaxed and head upright, with eyes gently lowered to be gazing at the space about three or four feet ahead of you. Allow your knees to bend naturally and your feet to greet the ground in a heel-to-toe action. Let the breath rise and fall calmly.
4. During the first circuit of the room bring to mind the two words that you focussed on from the text. With each step say one of the words silently in your mind so that the two words begin to accompany your two feet as they move forward in rhythm. Continue in this way until you have completed one circuit of the room.
5. For the second circuit of the room stop repeating the two words. Just notice how your body is, how your mind is, how the silence is.
6. For the third circuit of the room return to repeating the two words, one with each step.
7. Continue in this way, alternating between circuits with and without words. Notice if anything changes in your body, breath, mind, heart. Notice what arises. Notice what falls away.

8. Finish with a period of silence and stillness.

Other possibilities for walking meditation include walking a labyrinth, walking barefeet, walking outdoors in a garden, walking with eyes closed and a partner accompanying, walking with music.

## Find out more

- Thich Nhat Hanh. *The long road turns to joy: a guide to walking meditation.* Parallax Press, 1996 (walking meditation is also described in the author's other books listed on page 26).
- A virtual labyrinth with contemplative activities at points along the path at: www.rejesus.co.uk/site/module/labyrinth
- A walking meditation at: http://taoism.about.com/od/meditation/ht/walking.htm
- Walking meditation with Thich Nhat Hanh on You Tube at: www.youtube.com/watch?v=QdO1vZJgUu0 (or search for 'Walking Meditation with Thich Nhat Hanh' at www.youtube.com).

# Worship workshop guidelines

## The Kindlers' Laboratories of the Spirit

Kindlers' projects aim for participants to be engaged in exploring together matters that are eternal. Interactive processes help bond the community so that it will be moved to witness more powerfully: 'from worship to community to witness'. Silent Sunday worship unites us in spirit but not in fellowship: coffee and chat afterwards is not sufficient to get to know each other in any depth. Worship workshops complement Sunday meetings.

A worship workshop can take innumerable forms and each Kindlers project is another experiment. In this sense the meeting becomes a laboratory. What follows is open-ended and adaptable to any content or spiritual practice, following a simple pattern that is easy to facilitate. There are three dimensions (with timings for a two-hour workshop):

1. A Go-Round involving the whole group (30 mins)
2. Stimulus (15/20 mins), then pair work, small groups, and plenary (40/45 mins)
3. Worship, often of a more experimental kind (30 mins).

## A Go-Round

*This introduction may be read by the session facilitator following any welcome and general introduction.*

"Each evening we shall begin with a sharing by all the members of the group in turn, to hear something of their experiences of the theme for the evening. It is a way of learning from each other about the variety of spiritual practices within the group and of getting to know each other. The invitation is to be honest; not to be shy of what we can affirm and celebrate, nor be ashamed of what we find difficult and feel we have failed in.

We shall go round the group as we sit, starting each week with a different person, and I shall be part of that. In the weeks to come you might like to think ahead of what you want to share, as we have just about 25 minutes [give an indication of how many minutes for each person to speak]. I will indicate if someone is taking too long.

We must be accepting of whatever anybody shares; there is no dialogue, questioning or putting anyone down. If we have time at the end of a Go-Round we might pick up any common threads or tangles for us to unravel later. Tonight, let's start with [name]."

*This breaks the ice, means that everyone has been heard and everyone will gain in confidence over the series of sessions.*

## The stimulus

The overall theme of your series of sessions could be one of a thousand different matters that will already have been announced by the programme group, elders or organisers. Key issues at the heart of worship are prayer, God, Jesus, Christ, compassion, forgiveness, Light, darkness, death, rebirth. 15–20 minutes is long enough if the input is well presented, clear and succinct. Examples of input are: a talk, a dialogue between two Friends, a structured exercise, a DVD, an activity.

### Response and involvement

Working in pairs for 5–10 minutes, with the facilitator making up any uneven number, is one of the best ways for everybody to begin to engage with the topic. Then, it is good to work with a different partner and explore a contrary aspect for a second 5–10 minutes. This might then lead into groups of four, considering another facet of the issue, and conclude with a plenary time for everyone in a circle.

### Double circle exercise

Another lively way into the topic is the double circle exercise.

- Set up the group in two circles of chairs, an inner and outer circle, with partners knee to knee facing each other – the facilitator making up any odd number. Friends who are not too mobile can be on the inner circle, which need not then move.
- A quick way of getting into this format is to label everyone in the whole circle, 'A' or 'B', then ask the As to move their chairs round to face the person B on their right and sit closely, knee to knee, so that partners can talk easily to each other.
- The facilitator has worked out maybe 10 or 12 different questions about the topic chosen. They ask the first question to all the Bs, the outer circle. For one minute the Bs then give a response to A, and after a minute both can go into dialogue for a second minute.

- Then the facilitator gives all the As, the inner circle, a different question. For a minute As respond to Bs, then go into dialogue. After two minutes the Bs are asked to stand up and move clockwise to the next chair in their circle, so sitting opposite a new A.
- Then the As are asked a third question and respond (2 mins) and Bs asked a fourth question and respond (2 mins). After the fourth question, all the Bs stand again and move one seat clockwise. And so forth.

This exercise benefits from lively, accessible and challenging questions from the facilitator. Friends enjoy working with different Friends as they go round. Dialogues are tasters into the core of the matter. Ten questions will take about 25 minutes and then the group will be ready to come back into a final plenary whole circle to consolidate.

## Experimental worship

Worship is often much deeper when it comes after a time of enjoyable, social interaction that touches on crucial areas of faith, belief and understanding, as experienced in the first two stages of the workshop.

The group may be ready to express themselves in different ways in worship – through Taize-type song, meditative circle dance, poetry or readings and silence, creative listening, passing a symbolic object round the circle, witnessing, worship sharing, as well as contemplation without ministry, and traditional Quaker worship. The conclusion may be the group joining hands for a while. Then the theme for the next week is announced, so that spiritual preparation is invited. Finally, an encouragement to Live in the Life is vital.

## Living in the Life

It is helpful to offer an invitation to those about to start any worship workshops programme to make a resolve, at least for the period of the programme, for Friends to enrich their daily spiritual practice, however briefly, and to set about something fresh and new.

To **Live the Life** in the Quaker Way is for each Friend to find spiritual practices that they are most comfortable with in the hurly-burly of everyday life. The aim is to affirm the sacred in whatever we do. There is no part of our mundane reality that is not irradiated with divinity, but in the hourly stress and busyness of coping with a multitude of tasks the sense of holiness and wholeness inevitably gets swamped. The discipline of daily and weekly practices helps us to hold on to the other dimension, come what may. It is best if these practices are not followed too obsessively, so that they become a duty rather than an enjoyment. Yet a degree of discipline is necessary, as other priorities inevitably intrude. What we choose to do is highly personal and depends on what makes for a balanced life.

## Find out more

- Brown, Elizabeth and Alec Davison, eds. *Journeying the Heartlands: exploring spiritual practices of Quaker worship*. The Kindlers, 2010.
- Jarman, Roswitha. *Breakthrough to Unity: the Quaker Way held within the mystic traditions*. The Kindlers, 2010.
- Parkinson, Frank. *The Power we call God: threshings matter for Quaker visioning*. Kindlers, 2011.
- Parr, Peter. *Answering that of God*. Quaker Books, 2012.

# Endnotes

1   *Quaker faith & practice*, 23.02
2   Richard Rohr.
3   quoted in Margery Post Abbott, *To be Broken & Tender: a Quaker Theology for Today* [Whittier CA] (Friend Bulletin Corporation, 2010), p. 141.
4   quoted in Doug Gwyn, *Conversations with Christ* (FGC Quaker Press, 2011), p. 52.
5   quoted in Melvyn Matthews, *Both Alike to Thee* (SPCK Publishing), p. 102.
6   Richard Rohr, quoted in Brian McClaren, *Naked Spirituality* (Hodder & Stoughton, 2011), p. 213.
7   Anthony de Mello in *Sadhana: a way to God*, p. 47.
8   Hugo Rahner.

# Appendix:
# General resources for
# deepening the life of the Spirit

The books and web links listed below are general resources on prayer and spiritual practice, or cover practices not included in this book. Resources relating to specific practices described in this book are listed in the relevant section.

## Books

- Allen, Beth. *Ground and spring: foundations of Quaker discipleship*. Quaker Books, 2007.
- Birkel, Michael. *Silence and Witness: the Quaker tradition*. DLT, 2004.
- Brown Taylor, Barbara. *An Altar in the World: finding the sacred beneath our feet*. Canterbury Press, 2009.
- Cadman, David. *Holiness in the everyday*. Quaker Books, 2009.
- Cotter, Jim & Paul Paynton. *Out of the silence... Into the silence: prayer's daily round*. Cairns Publications, 2006.
- de Mello, Anthony. *Sadhana: a way to God – Christian exercises in eastern form*. Bantam Doubleday Dell, 1978.
- Gardner, Curt. *God just is: approaches to silent worship*. Quaker Books, 2012.
- Griffin, Emilie. *Doors into prayer*. DLT, 2003.
- Harvey, Ruth. *Wrestling and Resting: exploring stories of spirituality from Britain and Ireland*. CCBI, 2000.
- Holdsworth, Christopher. *Steps in a Large Room*. Quaker Books, 2007 (Swarthmore Lecture 1985).
- Holmgaard, Elisabeth. *'Be still and know that I am God': thoughts on prayer*. Woodbrooke, 1984.
- Hughes, Gerard. *God in All Things*. Hodder & Stoughton, 2004.
- Hughes, Gerard. *God of Surprises*. DLT, 1985.
- Jamison, Christopher. *Finding Sanctuary: monastic steps for everyday life*. Phoenix, 2007.
- Keane, Sheila. *Prayer: beginning again* (Pendle Hill pamphlet). Pendle Hill, 1998.
- Kelly, Thomas R. *A Testament of Devotion*. Harper & Row, 1939.
- Lacout, Pierre. *God is Silence*. Quaker Books, 1970.
- Laird, Martin. *Into the Silent Land*. DLT, 2006.

- Loring, Patricia. *Listening Spirituality Volume 1: personal spiritual practices among Friends.* Openings Press, 1997.
- Loring, Patricia. *Listening Spirituality Volume 2: corporate spiritual practice among Friends.* Openings Press, 1997.
- Main, John. *Word into silence: a manual for Christian meditation.* Canterbury Press, 2006.
- Mayfield, Sue. *Exploring prayer.* Lion Hudson, 2007.
- Merton, Thomas. *Contemplative prayer.* DLT, 2005.
- Morgan, Henry and Roy Gregory. *The God you already know: developing your spiritual and prayer life.* SPCK, 2009.
- Nicholl, Donald. *Holiness.* DLT, 2004.
- Norris, Gunilla and Greta Sibley. *Being home: discovering the spiritual in the everyday.* HiddenSpring, 2002.
- Pym, Jim. *You don't have to sit on the floor: making Buddhism part of your everyday life.* Amorata Press, 2002.
- *Quaker faith & practice.* Quaker Books, 2009 (4th edition).
- Roberts, Elizabeth and Elias Amidon, eds. *Earth Prayers from Around the World.* HarperCollins, 1991.
- Rohr, Richard. *Everything Belongs: the gift of contemplative prayer.* Crossroad Publishing, 2003.
- Silf, Margaret. *Taste and See: adventuring into prayer.* DLT, 1999. (Or any of her other books on prayer.)
- Slee, Nicola. *Praying Like a Woman.* SPCK, 2004.
- Small, Simon. *From the Bottom of the Pond: the forgotten art of experiencing God in the depths of the present moment.* O Books, 2007.
- Steindl-Rast, David. *A Listening Heart: the art of contemplation.* Crossroads, 1999.
- Steven, Helen. *No Extraordinary Power: prayer, stillness and activism* (Swarthmore Lecture 2005). Quaker Books, 2005.
- Tanner, Anne. *Practical prayer: making space for God in everyday life.* ABC, 2001.
- Walsh, Roger. *Essential Spirituality: exercises from the world's religions to cultivate kindness, love, joy, peace, wisdom and generosity.* Wiley & Sons, 1999.
- Whitmire, Catherine. *Plain Living: a Quaker path to simplicity.* Ave Maria Press, 2001.
- Woodhouse, Patrick. *Beyond words: an introduction, guide and resource for a contemplative way of prayer.* Kevin Mayhew, 2001.

# Links

- Buddhist 'Pebble for your pocket' meditation from Thich Naht Hanh's Plum Village monastery at: www.youtube.com/watch?v=TXJs9bdcnXw
  (or search for 'Pebble for your pocket Meditation' at: www.youtube.com)
- Christian meditation guidance and talks on You Tube at: www.youtube.com/user/meditatiowccm
- A contemplative mind mapping exercise at: http://loyolahall.co.uk/spirituality/praying-contemplative-mindmapping
- Daily prayer based on short Bible readings at: http://sacredspace.ie
- Daily prayer download with brief scripture readings and reflective questions at: www.pray-as-you-go.org
- Modern icons that could be used in contemplation (including Quaker martyr Mary Dyer) at: www.fatherbill.org/gallery.php
- Prayer and spirituality links (largely Christian) at: www.prayingeachday.org/prayersites.html
- Prayers from many traditions (a searchable collection) at: www.worldprayers.org/index.html
- Quaker meeting for worship online at: www.quakerworship.org/default.asp
- Taize chants and prayers to listen to or download at: www.taize.fr/en_article681.html
- A virtual labyrinth with contemplative activities at points along the path at: www.rejesus.co.uk/site/module/labyrinth
- Writing your own psalm to pray with at: http://loyolahall.co.uk/spirituality/a-way-of-praying-your-personal-psalm